PALEO POWER LUNCH

EASY, FILLING, & DELICOUS WORKDAY MEAL STRATEGIES

By Stormy Sweitzer

Foreword by Melissa Joulwan

Maoomba

Salt Lake City, UT

Maoomba, LLC
PO Box 91065
Salt Lake City, UT 84109

Photographs and book design by Stormy Sweitzer

Sweitzer, Stormy, 1974-.
Paleo Power Lunch: Easy, filling, & delicious workday meal strategies / Stormy Sweitzer; foreword by Melissa Joulwan.

Includes index.

ISBN-13: 978-0615629537 (Maoomba)

ISBN-10: 0615629539

To Will for his unflagging support and to my wonderful family for always believing in me.

CONTENTS

FOREWORD

Eating Paleo is often defined by the things we give up, so it's always refreshing to find someone who opens up our minds to the vast, delicious possibilities of meat, vegetables, fruits, and fats.

With her charming, effective cookbook, Stormy Sweitzer completely redefines the phrase "power lunch." Forget about professionals taking deals and making calls from the corner table of a swank dining room. These are real power lunches: meals packed with body-building protein, vibrant produce, luscious nuts and oils, and — most importantly — flavors that will satisfy your taste buds and make it easy to be true to your healthy habits.

More than a cookbook, Paleo Power Lunch is a how-to guide for creating easy-to-make, easy-to-transport meals that will make lunch a welcome respite in the middle of a busy work day — whether you're in a corporate office or CEO of your household.

The basis of the Power Lunch is a salad. But forget about bowls of tired greens and grilled chicken. Stormy's vibrant salad ideas combine elements of sweet and savory, chewy and crisp, all-American and international — along with homemade dressings of endless variations. With Stormy's simple instructions, even cooks with limited kitchen experience will be Paleo power players.

But it's not just about the recipes. Drawing on her own experience, Stormy goes beyond recipes to teach you real-life strategies for shopping, prepping, and packing your food. The pages are bursting with helpful tips to minimize prep time so you can make the most of meal time. There's a handy chart to help you plan weekly meals, along with advice on the science of packing to keep your Power Lunch fresh and crisp.

The recipes in Paleo Power Lunch will feed your imagination and your body, and the helpful tips will simplify the logistics of keeping your good health habits, even when you're eating away from home.

--Melissa Joulwan, author of *Well Fed: Paleo Recipes for People Who Love to Eat* and The Clothes Make The Girl Blog

INTRODUCTION

How often do you go to work, only to find that your schedule changes and you don't have a lot of time – if any – for lunch? Or you get so engrossed in what you are doing that you only come up for air when you are shaky and just need food now? What do you do?

- Buy a wilted salad with who-knows-what's-in-it dressing from a nearby store?

- Grab and gorge on sugary snacks from the vending machine or the stale almonds you've squirreled away for emergencies?

- Hit a drive-through and wind up with a headache or feeling like a slug the rest of the afternoon?

- Or, not eat lunch at all?

By the end of the day, you are grouchy, tired, unfocused, and maybe even feel ill. And, if you haven't gone to the gym yet, you've probably lost your motivation to go.

As someone who has had her share of long work-days and a desire to balance them with exercise, family time, and all of the other things I love to do, I understand the need for healthy, affordable, and filling lunch ideas that I can quickly prepare and eat no matter what kind of day I'm facing.

LUNCH IN A NUTSHELL

Paleo Power Lunch is not just another recipe book. It includes strategies for eating better, ideas for shopping creatively and efficiently, tips for storing and packing ingredients and lunches, and a system for preparing great lunches using recipes in the book or the ingredients you have on hand.

Each chapter in this book reflects a step in making your Paleo Power Lunch:

1. Plan for the week and shop for what you need

2. Prepare cooked and fresh ingredients

3. Make dressing in advance

4. Create powerful lunch combinations

5. Pack your lunch and the snacks you will need to face the day

As someone with numerous food sensitivities and a desire to eat real foods that support my health and fitness goals, I also want access to meals that taste good, meet my dietary needs, and give me energy throughout the day.

Paleo Power Lunches are some of the best ways I've come up with to stick to my healthy food choices in a culture where it's far easier to just grab a cheeseburger and fries.

What's a Paleo Power Lunch, you ask? At its core, it is a salad – using salad greens, vegetables, and dressing.

But these are no ordinary salads. In fact, Paleo Power Lunches defy the traditional notion of a salad by playing center stage – no side action here – and by changing toppings from a decoration to the highlight of the meal.

By using meats, poultry and seafood, nuts and seeds, and other hearty ingredients, Paleo Power Lunches turn a salad into a meal that is filling, satisfying, and flavorful. And, above all, easy to prepare and pack for whatever your day throws at you.

Paleo Power Lunch is designed to help you:

- Find creative and easy ways to make meals that use Paleo diet principles and real food ingredients

- Feel better by avoiding grains (including those with gluten), dairy, legumes, sugar and processed ingredients

- Manage time and money spent preparing lunches

- Support your health and fitness goals, while also keeping you sharp throughout the day

HOW DID I GET HERE?

For me, eating a more traditional diet is a way that I am able to manage multiple food sensitivities, maintain long term health goals, and power my active life. In many ways, it is also a return to my childhood.

I was fortunate to have grown up in a rural community, eating garden-fresh vegetables, fruit from the orchards behind our house, and locally-raised meats and wild game, as well as the traditional Mexican food that my mom made – not the cheesy, lettucey restaurant food that often passes for Mexican. It all seems very idyllic, but the truth is, my family also ate a lot of the processed foods that were popular in the 70s and 80s – the ones we now rail against, but loved as kids.

In my late teens and early 20s, I had opportunity to travel, spending 4 years studying and working abroad. My tastes were greatly influenced by the exotic flavors, new-to-me ingredients, and cooking styles I found along the way. I took up weight-lifting, cycling and running – at first casually, and then more diligently, riding in long-distance events and participating in several half-marathons a year.

Settling back in the States, I worked as a project manager and consultant (focusing on systems, processes, and data) in the nonprofit and health care sectors for many years. A lot of my work focused on creating ways for physicians to help their patients prevent diabetes and heart disease and better manage chronic illness. I saw the effects of poor diet and no exercise on these patients, but found myself adding more and more processed and fast foods to my own diet as life got busier and I spent more time on the road.

For a long time, things were fine. Unfortunately, they took a turn for the worse several years ago.

I suddenly started developing inexplicable health problems – hair loss, rosacea, weight gain, energy loss, even mild depression. Doctors told me I was fine physically and that I just needed less stress in my life. The thing is, I didn't feel anymore stressed than usual, and I didn't trust that the tests were giving me the answers I needed.

A book on improving metabolic function that I checked out of the library turned out to be about the potentially-negative impacts of certain foods. One chapter described all of my symptoms to a T. The next day, I started the recommended elimination diet and came to the realization that gluten and dairy were wreaking havoc on me. A blood test confirmed these and other food sensitivities.

Within one month of switching to an ancestral food diet that included meats, fish, fresh fruits and vegetables, nut and seeds – and excluded dairy, gluten (and most other grains), yeast, and sugar – I was a new woman. The weight came off, all of my symptoms disappeared, and I felt more energetic than I had in a long time. In addition to feeling better, my running performance improved. That was all the proof I needed that food was the way to better health.

Despite these great results, overhauling my diet wasn't easy. To manage my allergies, I HAD to avoid particular foods to feel good; my husband didn't need to change a thing (so he thought). It took a year for us to migrate to a unified kitchen that focused on allergen-free foods, and a couple of years more to realize that the baked good alternatives and sugary foods I occasionally ate – despite being gluten, yeast, and dairy-free – were not doing me any favors. It was time to just eat real food.

Preparing whole foods took longer than I was used to and it took me a while to find ways to be efficient with my shopping and cooking. Trying to find good food on the go – especially during the work day, when traveling, or heading out for a long run – was especially hard.

It wasn't until I shifted my mindset to one of WANT, that things became easier. Who doesn't want to be healthy, to feel good and strong, to eat fantastic food, to have energy and time for all of the things they want to do in life?

This desire motivated me to come up with strategies to make things easier for myself and drew on my childhood love of fruits and vegetables and my adventurer's love of culinary experimentation.

The strategies behind these meals were some of the first I developed to manage my food goals and needs. While I wasn't aware of the Paleo diet when I first came up with these lunch recipes, intuitively, I followed the same principles.

I hope you will enjoy them and build on them to make your own powerful lunch creations.

WHAT IS THE PALEO WAY OF EATING?

The modern Paleo (from the word Paleolithic) diet is an approach to eating that is based on evolutionary science and the idea that human metabolic and digestive function have not evolved at the same pace as our agricultural innovation. In short: we are not able to easily absorb nutrients from many of the food products available to us today. While we now live in times when we are more likely to shop and consume, the Paleo way of eating encourages a diet that is more akin to the plant and pastured animal-based diet our distant ancestors ate, but using select, currently-available real foods.

The diet consists primarily of meat – preferably grass-fed beef, lamb and pork, free range poultry, eggs, wild game, fish and other seafood, vegetables, fruit, seeds, and nuts. It emphasizes high-quality nutrients, healthy proteins, complex carbohydrates, and good fats. Think of it as real food that comes from as close to the source as possible.

It excludes cereal grains and grain-like seeds (e.g., buckwheat, amaranth, quinoa), legumes (beans, lentils, chickpeas, green peas, peanuts, etc.), dairy products, salt, refined sugar and sweets, and unhealthy cooking oils, as well as processed meats. These foods, and lack of healthy foods, have been found to contribute to any number of allergies, auto-immune disorders, and chronic illnesses like diabetes and heart disease.

Because food is central to so many aspects of health, people come to the Paleo diet from all walks of life. Many choose to eat Paleo foods to support fitness and weight goals. Some choose Paleo as a next step in their quest to manage food allergies or disease. And still others see it as a way to commit to a lifetime of healthy, whole foods that avoid processed ingredients, additives and fillers.

While eating this way may, at first, seem limiting compared to most things we eat today, the Paleo diet is actually luxurious...luxurious in its real food flavors, textures, colors, aromas, variety, and the way food is prepared. But, being luxurious does not mean that following a Paleo diet has to be difficult, time-consuming or expensive.

With the right tools, information, and strategies, it is easier than ever to incorporate real food and workday meals into your already-full and active life.

CHAPTER ONE

GETTING READY

- TOOLS
- INGREDIENTS
- STOCKING YOUR KITCHEN

Paleo Power Lunches are designed to be quick and easy to put together just before you need them, but they do take some planning and preparation. The great thing is, there are tools and approaches you can use to develop a routine that makes the most of your time and budget, and keeps waste to a minimum.

- **Kitchen Tools** – The tools to prepare, store, and transport ingredients and completed meals to work.

- **Power Ingredients** – Paleo-approved ingredients, as well as foods to avoid.

- **Planning for the Week** – Strategies for menu planning and shopping that minimize waste.

- **Shopping Strategies** – Ways to shop effectively, where to shop, concerns for people with food allergies, and how to manage cost-time tradeoffs.

KITCHEN POWER TOOLS

To make your Paleo Power Lunch, you will need the right tools for the job – from tools to prepare and store ingredients to those needed for carrying your completed meals to work easily.

Some of the best kitchen tools are those that are straightforward and easy to use. If you have more advanced equipment, please feel free to use it.

Here are the basics I suggest:

Sauté pan – for pan-frying meats

Sauce pan / pot – to hard-boil eggs

Baking sheet – to roast vegetables and meat

Colander or salad mixer – for rinsing fresh produce

Small mixing bowl – for mixing up dressings

Whisk or mixing spoon – for mixing up dressings

Blender – for mixing up dressings

Measuring spoons and cups – to measure ingredients

Digital food scale – to help you gauge portion sizes

Meat thermometer – to check meat temperature for safety and doneness

Grater – to shred carrots and other veggies if you want

Sharp knives – to cut safely and easily; a chef's knife and a paring or utility knife are helpful

Citrus squeezer – to make it easier to squeeze out every last drop of juice

Glass jars or salad dressing bottles – to store your yummy dressings

1/2-ounce food storage containers – for packing dressings for each day

5- to 6-cup capacity lidded bowl or food storage container – to hold a single lunch

Other food storage containers of various sizes – for storing ingredients.

Lunch bag or cooler – to take your food where you need it

PALEO POWER INGREDIENTS – AN IDEA LIST

When it comes to eating the ancestral way, the key is to focus on all of the things you can eat, rather than the things you cannot. Focus on healthy proteins and fats, fresh fruits and vegetables, nuts and seeds, and fresh herbs and spices. Buy the highest quality you can afford.

While Paleo Power Lunch recipes use ingredients like the ones listed below, there are many, many more Paleo-inspired options you could add to your diet.

PROTEINS

Wild Game – cuts of venison or bison or other available game meats

Grass-fed Beef
- flank steak
- sirloin
- London broil
- chuck steak

Free-range Poultry & Eggs
- turkey breast or loin
- chicken breast

Pasture-raised Pork
- loin
- chops
- roast
- bacon

Sustainably caught or farmed fish and seafood
- Ahi tuna
- Red snapper
- Salmon
- Tilapia
- Shrimp

LEAFY GREENS

Arugula
Beet greens*
Chicory*
Collards*
Dandelion greens
Endive
Escarole*
Kale*
Lettuce
Mache
Mustard greens*
Radicchio
Rocket
Romaine
Sorrel
Spinach
Spring greens mix
Swiss chard*
Turnip greens*
Watercress

*Taste better cooked

VEGETABLES

Asparagus
Beets
Broccoli
Brussels sprouts
Cabbage
Carrots
Cauliflower
Celery
Cucumber
Eggplant
Green onions
Green peppers
Mushrooms
Onion
Red peppers
Pumpkin
Radish
Sea vegetables
Squash
Sweet potatoes
Tomatoes
Yams
Zucchini

FRESH FRUIT

There are hundreds of different types of fruit that could be used. These are some of the most commonly-available.

Apples
Apricots
Avocados
Bananas
Blackberries
Blueberries
Cantaloupe
Cherries
Cranberries
Figs (fresh)
Grapefruit
Grapes
Honeydew melon
Lemons
Limes
Mangos
Nectarines
Oranges
Peaches
Pears
Pineapple
Plums
Pomegranates
Pomelo (AKA Pummelo)
Raspberries
Strawberries
Watermelon

NUTS AND SEEDS

Almonds (and Almond Butter)
Brazil
Cashews
Chestnuts
Hazelnuts
Macadamia nuts
Pecans
Pine nuts
Pistachios
Pepitas (AKA raw pumpkin seeds
Sesame seeds
Sunflower seeds
Walnuts

FRESH HERBS

If you don't have access to fresh, dried will typically do in dressings.

Basil
Chives
Cilantro
Dill
Fennel
Garlic
Ginger
Mint
Oregano
Parsley
Rosemary
Tarragon
Thyme

SPICES

Black pepper
Chile powder
Chile flakes
Cinnamon
Cloves
Cocoa powder
Coriander
Cumin
Curry powder
Jamaican jerk seasoning blend (salt-free)
Mustard powder
Turmeric
Wasabi powder

OILS

Avocado oil
Flax seed oil
Olive oil (extra-virgin)
Walnut oil
Coconut oil
Melted bacon fat

OTHER

Apple cider vinegar
Balsamic vinegar
Red/white wine vinegar
Liquid coconut aminos
Raw honey

FOODS TO AVOID

Focusing on what you can eat is a helpful way to create delicious and satisfying Paleo meals. Sometimes, though, we are faced with foods and ingredients that are not ancestrally-inspired – such as sugary foods, foods that contain unhealthy fats and high amounts of sodium, and foods that contain antinutrients that prevent us from absorbing a food's full nutritional value. Many of these foods have been found to contribute to poor health and are best avoided.

Here are items you should try to avoid.

- Legumes, including beans, lentils, chickpeas, peanuts, etc.

- Dairy products

- Cereal grains, including wheat and all other grains and grain-like seeds (i.e., amaranth, buckwheat, quinoa)

- Salt and sugar

- Baked goods and deep-fried foods

- Processed foods, including commercial dressings

- Soda

PLANNING FOR THE WEEK

All too often, we go shopping without a plan. When we do that, we're very likely to wind up with lots of different ingredients that don't really go together, or we get grand ideas, but don't have the time to put them into action before things wilt and rot. Either way, we run the risk of not having the meals we'd hoped for and end up wasting both food and money.

One of the best ways to avoid this situation is to write down what you plan to eat during the week. Doing this can help you come up with a menu that makes the most of your time, tastes, and budget, and which helps you become a more efficient shopper. You will also minimize food waste as you learn what gets eaten in your household and what does not.

Here are some ideas for getting started:

Think Big Picture: Think beyond lunch. Plan for all meals that you, and any others in your household, will eat during the week. Don't buy more fresh ingredients than what you'll eat. Don't worry if you don't get it right at first – by planning and monitoring what you buy versus what you eat, you'll soon get a feel for the quantities of food you need for a week.

Figure Out the Details: Think about whole meals. What ingredients make up a lunch or dinner? What foods go well together or taste good to you? Did you plan for in-between and on-the-go times, to make sure you have snacks and emergency foods on hand when you need them?

Plan Your Lunch Flow for the Week: Decide which meals you will eat during the week and shop for the fresh ingredients you will need for those meals. Choose Paleo Power Lunches that use the same leafy greens or dressing, for example, or to which you can add leftovers. Feel free to mix and match, using what you have on hand.

Make the Most of Your Time: Consider how ingredients can be used over multiple meals and create a *planned leftovers strategy*. In other words, prepare extra meat, poultry or seafood at dinner so you can use it in the next day's lunch. Or, take advantage of meal preparation time to chop up more vegetables than you need right now so you can use them in your Paleo Power Lunch or another meal later.

Be Flexible: Nothing can stop you in your tracks faster than feeling like you have to follow a plan. To keep things interesting and manageable, just remember to change up your meals and snacks if you find yourself getting bored and to simplify what you are doing if it feels overwhelming. If you crave foods that are better suited to the season or your activities, make something that satisfies you.

Consider Using What You Have: When planning out the week, think about what foods are sitting in your freezer or are still fresh in the fridge. Use them as soon as you can before buying additional groceries.

Quick Tip:

Make it Visible: Print your plan or write it on a white board in your kitchen to help keep track of your plans for the week.

WEEKLY MEAL PLAN

Meal	Monday	Tuesday	Wednesday	Thursday	Friday	Saturday	Sunday
Breakfast							
Snack							
Lunch							
Snack							
Dinner							
Other							

Notes: _____

_____

_____

OTHER BENEFITS OF TRACKING YOUR MEALS

You can use the planning grid to help you figure out your shopping list for the week, and you can also use it to track what you actually eat. Not only does it make your eating habits visible to you, it gives you a chance to look back on what you've eaten and use the information in a variety of ways.

Consider tracking what you eat and adding helpful notes:

- Compare what you planned to eat with what you actually ate – did you follow through with your plan, or did something take you off track?

- Note whether you liked a meal or not – and maybe what you would do to change it. This might cause you to improve your meal planning and shopping in the future.

- Learn your flavor combinations so you are better prepared to throw together a quick odds and ends lunch using whatever you have on hand.

- Track how foods make you feel. This is particularly helpful in understanding how food affects your mood, energy levels, and whether you have allergies or sensitivities to certain foods. Keep in mind that reactions may take a couple of days to show up.

- Count calorie intake or the protein-carbohydrate-fat distribution of your food to see how they affect your weight and physical activity. Many people who follow a Paleo diet do not track calories, because they are eating good, wholesome food. Despite this, tracking what you eat can be helpful if you are trying to achieve a particular weight or nutrient intake.

A simple notebook or tracking sheet, like the example shared in this book, can be helpful for jotting things throughout the day. There are also a number of food-tracking programs – including Paleo-specific – available online to help you monitor the foods you eat and the calories they provide.

AVOIDING BOREDOM

While there are numerous possible Paleo Power Lunch combinations, it can be good to break things up during the week so that you don't get bored.

Use variety as your guide when planning out the week:

- Mix and match your Paleo Power Lunches
- Use herbs and spices liberally – they add flavor to a meal
- Make a pot of soup or stew – store some in the fridge and freeze the rest in serving size containers
- Roast or grill a few extra servings of meat or make more of whatever else you are having for dinner to take as leftovers the next day
- Spend a day once a month making your own frozen lunches – pull them out when you don't feel like cooking
- Trade meals with friends that have a similar eating ethic
- And, if you decide to go out to eat, go to a restaurant with healthy options

BECOME A STRATEGIC GROCERY SHOPPER

Shopping the Paleo way is actually incredibly easy. Nonetheless, there are different places and ways to shop that can get you more bang for your buck, save you time in the kitchen, and ensure that you make food selections that are fresh, raised in the most healthful way, are safe for any food allergies or sensitivities you might have, and which add variety to your plate and palate.

FRINGE SHOPPING

Nearly all of the foods you will eat on a Paleo-inspired diet are stocked in the fringe – or outer edges – of typical grocery stores: the fresh produce section, egg fridge, butchery, and bulk food section. The inner aisles are helpful for oils, frozen foods, and packaged nuts and seeds.

1. Shop around the outer edges of your store in the meat and produce sections.

2. Drop by the frozen food aisle for fruits and vegetables that are not available fresh.

3. Seek out bottled spices, packaged nuts and seeds, and healthy oils from the baking, bulk or health food sections.

4. Be sure to read food labels – if the items you've selected have labels – and aim for items that do not include foods you have allergies to or unnecessary sugars, salt or preservatives.

5. Head to check-out!

BEYOND THE GROCERY STORE

Don't feel locked down by your grocery store – whether chain or local. It is just one of many places you can find great food for the week.

- **Local markets and health food stores:** Visit these stores for organic and local produce, pasture-raised meats, organic canned and frozen goods, and specialty items.

- **Ethnic grocery stores:** You can find spices, special sauces, and fresh herbs at your grocery store, but sometimes the ethnic stores are more affordable, have a greater variety, and offer unique fresh herbs, fruits and vegetables, to boot. Don't know what something is? Ask. Most proprietors want your business and are happy to tell you what things are and how to use them in your cooking.

- **Food co-op or community-supported agriculture (CSA) program:** If you want a reliable supply of varied fruits, vegetables, and other locally-produced foods, join a co-op or CSA. With a co-op, you can often offset the cost of food or membership by volunteering. With a CSA, you pay for a share or more of garden goodies up front and receive a set amount of whatever is in season each week throughout the growing season. If ever there were a way to keep your meals fresh while keeping you on your toes, this is it.

- **Farmer's market:** Many cities now offer farmer's markets where local food producers bring their freshly-picked, seasonal fruits, vegetables, and herbs, as well as meats, eggs, and cottage foods. They are a great place to find fresh, tasty food, and you get to meet the people who grow and raise it.

- **Local farms and ranches:** Today, many farmers and ranchers offer UPick and direct to purchaser options. You can visit the farm – or they deliver to a central location – to pick up the grass-fed beef, free-range chicken, or organic produce you've purchased from them. In some cases, you can buy a large quantity, such as a side of beef, and freeze it for access throughout the year. Worried that you can't eat it all? Split the cost with friends and share.

- **Grow your own:** Feeling adventurous? Try growing your own food. Tomatoes, herbs, and greens can be grown easily in small areas and containers.

STOCK VS. SHOP

Ingredients typically fall into two categories: those you should buy fresh or frozen and those you should stock up on in your pantry or freezer so that you always have good food on hand.

- **Buy Fresh or Frozen:** Buy fresh fruits and vegetables, herbs, salad greens, and meat, poultry, and seafood fresh and use them quickly to get the best flavor. Frozen vegetables and fruit are a great alternative to fresh because they are picked ripe and immediately frozen, sealing in nutrients; look for ones that do not include extra sugar, salt, or additives.

- **Buy Fresh & Freeze:** Freeze meat, poultry, and seafood if you buy it in bulk and don't plan to use it right away.

- **Stock:** Stock your pantry with staples that store well and that you will use regularly. Staples include raw nuts and seeds, dried herbs, spices, oils, and vinegars.

TRADING OFF TIME AND MONEY

Time and money are critical issues when it comes to deciding what to eat. They are also highly personal. Only you know what you can afford and what your priorities are.

Generally speaking, to get the best flavor, the most nutrients, and the greatest health benefits from your food, **always buy the highest-quality ingredients you can afford**. One way to do this – to the extent you can afford it – is to purchase organic produce and sustainably-raised meats and caught fish. Fresh foods are also less-expensive when they are in season.

The decision about whether to eat out or make your own can also make a difference in your wallet and time. A restaurant lunch can cost you anywhere from $5 to $15 and up to an hour of your day. Making your own lunch can take some time in the morning or the night before, but, depending on the ingredients you choose, you will spend less and your lunch will be right there in your work place when you need it. You may even have time for a walk!

If you've already decided that making your own lunch is the way to go, then the real tradeoffs have to do with your shopping decisions and what you do in the kitchen.

Saving Time: If saving time is your priority, buy ingredients that have been cooked or cut for you (be sure to read the labels so you know what you're getting). Here are some examples:

- pre-washed salad greens
- shredded cabbage
- sliced mushrooms
- matchstick carrots
- chopped chicken breast
- pre-cooked turkey breast

- minced garlic and ginger
- fresh salsa from the refrigerator section
- fresh-sliced fruit
- fresh-sliced stir-fry vegetables
- slivered or chopped nuts

Ingredients like these will help save you time in the preparation step of your week. Keep in mind that you will typically pay extra for this convenience at the cash register.

Saving Money: To keep costs down, buy ingredients whole and raw, then cook, clean or otherwise prepare them yourself. This way, you aren't paying for extra packaging or convenience costs.

If you have the space for it, grow your own food. Even a simple kitchen herb garden or some potted tomatoes can give you delicious and affordable food.

Buying certain quantities of food can also save you money – such as purchasing a share in a CSA or splitting the cost of a cow with others. But if you don't eat them or freeze them right away, you can actually lose money and waste good food in the process.

Where you shop and whether you buy organic produce, pasture-raised meat, local eggs, etc. or buy conventionally grown and raised foods can also make a difference. While we all want to make the ideal purchases, sometimes we have to make purchases that are realistic for our budgets. Personally, I tend to eat more fruits and vegetables and less meat so I can afford the higher-quality meats I do buy.

A NOTE ON FOOD ALLERGIES AND SENSITIVITIES

Paleo eating naturally excludes several common food allergens – gluten; dairy proteins like lactose, casein and whey; soy; and peanuts; as well as grains and other foods that make it difficult for your body to absorb good nutrients.

By eating a diet of real, whole ingredients, you will avoid processed foods that pose a cross-contamination risk, and which are often high in sugars, sodium, commercial yeasts, gums, starches and food additives.

That said, if you have particular food allergies or sensitivities, the foods you can eat can still cause problems if they are cross-contaminated with foods you can't eat. This is particularly true with fresh meat and bulk foods.

Fresh cuts of meat, poultry, or fish that are stored in a butcher counter may or may not be separated from breaded, stuffed, or marinated cuts that include gluten or dairy ingredients. Buy your meats from a butcher that you know can tell you how the meats were prepared and which take care to separate items that pose a risk to you.

Nuts, seeds, dried fruit, and other dry goods that are available in bulk can be cross-contaminated through scoop-swapping and accidental spills from one bin to another. The information on how the foods were handled before arriving at the store can be vague or nonexistent. If you are allergic or highly sensitive, it may be best to buy what you need in packages that are clearly labeled with contents and manufacturing processes that support your food needs.

WASTE NOT, WANT NOT

Nobody likes to throw away food that's gone bad or waste money buying things that don't get eaten.

To keep waste to a minimum:

- Plan ahead and buy only what you expect to use – particularly fresh ingredients – during the next few days or week ahead.

- Life happens; if your work – or home – schedule changes and you know you won't be able to eat fresh ingredients before they go bad, cut and freeze them, make soup that can be frozen and eaten later, add extra fruits to a breakfast smoothie or vegetables to an omelet, or find someone else who can eat them while the goods are still good.

- If a food is new to you, buy just enough to try it and no more. If you don't like it, there will be nothing (or very little) to throw away.

- Home gardeners can turn uncooked, oil-free fruit and vegetable waste into compost.

- Raw beef bones, a chicken carcass, or shrimp shells can be simmered in water with onions, vegetables like carrots or celery, and herbs, to make a delicious pot of homemade soup stock.

Quick Tip: Track your food waste for a week.

Throughout the day, write down:

- What food you throw away.
- How much.
- Where (e.g., garbage, compost, give away).
- Why (e.g., served too much, tastes bad, ate lunch out, food has gone off).

Use the information to help you find ways to reduce waste, e.g., adjust serving sizes, what and how much food you buy, and how you prepare things.

Adapted from LoveFoodHateWaste.com

CHAPTER TWO

ADVANCE ACTION

PREPARING FOR THE WEEK AHEAD

Paleo Power Lunches are designed to be quick and easy to put together just before you need them. The key to making them quick and easy, though, is preparing food in advance. A game plan of focused preparation time and a planned leftover approach can help you pull lunch together in minutes.

Most preparation can be done on the weekend or the night before you need it. By getting in the habit of preparing ingredients, you will be more likely to put your lunch together throughout the week, rather than running out the door without it.

YOUR LUNCH PREPARATION GAME PLAN

Not everyone loves to plan, but it is good to have an idea of what's needed to get the job done – especially when time and follow-through are concerns.

The five things I think about when planning out my week are:

- What do I want to eat each day?

- Can I make something once and then use it in my lunches throughout the week?

- How can I break things up so I stay excited with my meals and maintain healthy habits?

- What can I make or prepare in advance that will save me time later?

- Will I really have time to make my lunch before work? If not, I'll pack it the night before.

The first three questions help with the meal planning and shopping covered in the last chapter. The last two help figure out when to set aside time to prepare ingredients in advance and to make lunch efficiently.

What do you do with this information? Put each of these steps in your calendar and make them a priority – just like anything else important to you.

You will need to spend some time planning (this gets easier), shopping, and an hour or so prepping your food for the week. Schedule these activities on days when you know you can make time for them. For most people – maybe you – the best time is one evening after work or on the weekend (or on whichever day you have off during the week).

CREATING YOUR GAME PLAN

Monday	Tuesday	Wednesday	Thursday	Friday	Saturday	Sunday
Take packed lunch	Make lunch in A.M. Make extras for leftovers + pack Wed lunch	Take packed lunch	Pull soup from freezer for lunch	Make Odds and Ends lunch in A.M.	Plan meals Shopping trip	1-2 hours prep time Pack Mon lunch

If it helps, add your game plan to a meal board. This could be a small white board in your kitchen, a standard calendar, or a printout of the meal planning sheet in the previous chapter. Write down what you will be eating each day and when you need to prepare your lunches. If you have a work lunch or are meeting someone on a particular day, add it to your plan.

As you can see from the example, there are a couple of ways to prepare:

1. **Set aside time on the weekend to prepare most** of what you'll need for lunches during the week. After you've decided what you want to eat for the coming week, do the prep work that makes sense - like chopping fresh vegetables, making salad dressing, and cooking up some meat and a soup. Then, throughout the week, you will only need to spend a few minutes putting your lunch together each day.

2. **Cook extra food at dinner** that you can use in your lunch the next day. It is often easier to add an extra chicken breast, steam or roast extra veggies, or boil extra eggs while you are already cooking, than it is to find extra time. Make a habit of cooking "planned leftovers" that you can easily add to your lunches throughout the week. Cook once, eat multiple times!

In the rest of the chapter, you'll find ways to take advance action and prepare some of the foods you'll need.

PROTEIN PREPARATIONS

There are many ways to prepare meat, poultry, and seafood. Whole books are written about each. I recommend you read one or two to learn more about how animals are raised, the different cuts you can use, and preparation techniques and safety.

Here are some of the basics and a couple of quick ways to prepare meat, poultry and seafood for the lunches in this book.

SOME TIPS TO GET YOU STARTED

Always preheat your pan, oven, or grill. In fact the secret to cooking with a stainless steel or cast iron pan is to get it hot before adding a single thing to it. The surface of the pan is altered by the heat and will prevent things from sticking.

Work with fresh or completely thawed meat, poultry, or fish. You can cook them if they are semi-frozen, but you will have to reduce the heat, move them further from the heat source, and cook them longer.

Braising is great for less-tender cuts of meat and game and is best done in a Dutch oven – in the oven – or a crock pot. Add 1/3 to 1/2 cup of liquid (stock or broth is great) and simmer at 325° to 350° F (163-177° C) or low heat setting until internal temperature tells you it's done.

COOK IT UP!

Braise: Brown meat and then slow cook it in liquid in a tightly-covered dish – use this to cook a larger cut of meat on the weekend

Broil: Cook fatty fish under high heat or finish a roast or braised meat this way to add color and texture to the surface

Grill*: Cook meat over high heat using a charcoal or gas grill or even fire

Poach: Gently simmer chicken, fish, or eggs in liquid

Roast*: Cook meat uncovered in the oven at 350° F (177° C) or above

Sauté*: Cook thinner cuts of meat in a shallow frying pan with a bit of melted fat of your choice (olive oil, bacon grease, coconut oil, etc.)

Stir-fry*: Cut meat into bite-sized pieces and quickly cook it with some melted fat over high heat

*Note: you can also use this technique to prepare vegetables.

THE PERFECT TEMPERATURE AND MORE

Internal temperature, texture, opaqueness, and color are signs of doneness. Learning what these signs are for each meat, poultry, and seafood type can make a difference in food safety, taste, preference, and how it feels in your mouth.

Achieving the perfect temperature is a matter of both safety and taste. These are safe minimum internal temperatures and signs of doneness recommended by the USDA.

Type of Meat	You know it's...	when...	and the internal temperature is...
Beef	Medium	center is light pink and outer area is brown	145° F /63° C
	Well Done	uniformly brown throughout	160°+ F / 72°+ C
Pork	Medium	pale pink center	145° F / 63° C
	Well Done	uniformly brown throughout	160°+ F / 72°+ C
Chicken & Turkey	Done	juices run clear	165°+ F / 72°+ C
Fish & Shellfish	Medium	flesh is opaque and flakes easily	145° F / 63° C

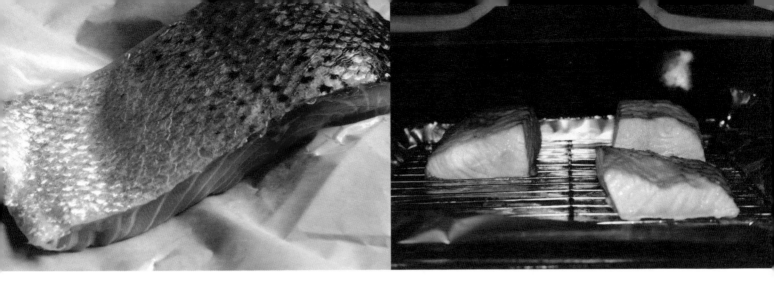

BROIL FISH

Set oven rack to the highest level. Preheat your oven to the broil setting.

Baste your fish with a little olive oil or melted coconut oil and lightly season it with salt, pepper, and other spices. You could also use the Basic Citrus Dressing on page 46 to baste the fish before broiling.

Place the fish on a greased broiler pan or cooking grate (skin-side-down if your fish has skin on it).

Put fish in the oven and broil for 3 to 5 minutes. Rotate and cook the fish for another 3 to 5 minutes.

Watch your fish closely; it will cook quickly. Thinner pieces may need to be removed from the oven earlier to avoid burning them. You will need to broil thicker cuts of fish longer.

Your fish is done when you can flake the thickest piece with a fork and the inside is opaque.

GRILL A CHICKEN BREAST

Preheat your grill to a medium flame or prepare wood or charcoal briquettes according to the instructions on the package.

Lightly coat the fresh chicken breast with olive oil. Season with salt, pepper, and garlic powder.

Place the chicken on the lower rack of your grill and cook for 8-10 minutes. Rotate breast and cook for 8-10 minutes longer. Adjust your cooking time if needed; thicker pieces will take longer to cook.

Cut into the thickest part of the breast to check for pinkness. If meat is white, you are good to go. If not, cook for a couple of minutes longer.

Remove chicken from heat and allow it to rest for a minute before slicing into strips or bite-sized pieces you can use in your lunch.

Want to throw something else on the grill? Try pork chops or tenderloin, steak, shrimp or chicken kabobs, or fish.

Quick Tip:

Do not puncture the flesh; keep it intact to seal in the juices.

POACH SHRIMP

Poaching shrimp is a great way to bring out its flavor, reduce fishiness, and keep it from drying out. Here is a method adapted from Lynne Rossetto Kasper's Weeknight Kitchen. You can also poach fish steaks and whole fish this way.

In a deep pot or pan, bring 2 inches of water or fish stock, 1 clove minced garlic, ½ teaspoon of salt, and a handful of fresh herbs – cilantro for the shrimp or dill, rosemary, or Italian parsley for fish – to a simmer. Cover the pot and let the liquid and herbs cook for 5 minutes.

When the liquid is ready, add the cleaned and deveined raw shrimp. Reduce the heat so the water barely trembles – this should be a gentle simmer, not a rolling boil. Cook the shrimp for about 2 minutes or until it is pink and cooked through. (For fish, poach for 8-10 minutes per inch of thickness.)

Transfer the poached shrimp or fish from the water onto a plate using a slotted spoon.

Quick Tip:

Try this with your favorite fish or seafood. For sustainable fish recommendations, visit the Monterrey Bay Aquarium Seafood Watch website.

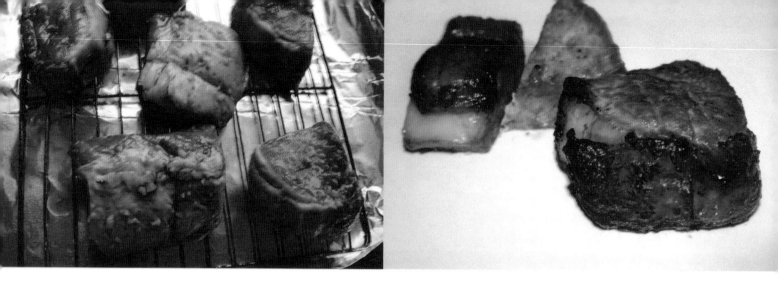

ROAST PORK LOIN

Cut a pork loin into 3-4" chunks. Do not remove excess fat. Brine your pork overnight using rock salt, herbs and citrus juice and rinds or marinate it using a Paleo marinade of your choice.

The next day, preheat your oven to 350° F (177° C).

Place the pork in a roasting pan or on a cooking grate in a foil-lined baking sheet.

Place pan on middle rack of oven and cook for 45 minutes to an hour (the larger the pieces of meat, the longer it will need to cook), rotating and basting the pork chunks with more marinade every 20 minutes. The pork is done when a thermometer reading from the center tells you it has reached the necessary internal temperature (~160° F for pork).

At the very end, coat the meat with one last layer of marinade and turn your oven to broil. Watch the meat quickly become crisp and golden.

Remove pork from heat and allow it to rest for at least 10 minutes before slicing it into strips or bite-sized pieces you can use in your lunch.

Prefer beef, whole chicken, a turkey breast, or wild game to pork? The process is basically the same. Simply adjust your cooking time and internal temperature; a whole chicken, for example, will take about 20 minutes per pound and will be done at 165° F.

PAN-FRY A PORK CHOP

Pan-frying is easiest with thinner cuts of meat (less than ¾" thick) – such as in the image on the upper right. With thicker cuts, you can simply put a lid on top, turn the temperature down, and cook the chop for longer. This allows the meat to cook thoroughly on the inside without burning on the outside.

Preheat your sauté pan to medium high heat. When hot, add a tablespoon of olive oil or your preferred cooking fat and coat the pan evenly.

Add your pork loin chop and reduce heat to medium. For a thin chop, cook for 2 minutes then flip the chop and cook for another 2 minutes. If you have a thicker chop, do the same thing, but then cover the pan with a lid, reduce the heat to low, and cook for an additional 5-7 minutes.

The pork should develop a beautiful golden crust to the outside. It is done when the thickest part of the pork chop is just white or the internal temperature is 160°F.

Let chops rest for 5-10 minutes before cutting into strips or bite-sized pieces.

Quick Tip:

To check if your pan is hot enough, add a teaspoon of water to it. If it balls up like mercury and ricochets around the pan, it is ready to go.

STIR-FRY BEEF STRIPS

When you are in a hurry or want to cook up some meat and vegetables together to add to your lunch, try stir-frying them.

Preheat your sauté pan to high heat. When hot, add a tablespoon of olive oil or your preferred cooking fat and coat the pan evenly.

Add aromatics, like onion, garlic or ginger. Stir frequently to keep things from burning. Cook until translucent (they will start to look clear), then add beef strips. Cook for about 2 minutes. Add any other vegetables you would like to stir-fry and cook until everything is done. The meat should be cooked through and vegetables tender.

Let cool and add the stir-fried food to a container separate from the rest of your Paleo Power Lunch ingredients. This way, you can reheat it before mixing it with raw lunch ingredients.

Stir-frying can also be done with bite-size or strip-cut chicken, pork, and seafood like shrimp and squid tubes, as well as quick-cooking vegetables like onions, peppers, zucchini, shredded cabbage and carrots.

HARD-BOIL EGGS

There are many ways to hard cook an egg – some people like to bake them, I prefer to boil them. Here is the best way I know.

Place several eggs in a heavy saucepan.

Add enough water to cover the eggs completely – 1 ½ to 2" of extra water above the egg line.

Bring the water to a boil and immediately remove the pan from the heat.

Cover the saucepan and let it stand for 10 minutes.

Cool the eggs in a bowl of ice water.

Refrigerate until you need them.

PREPARING FRESH PRODUCE

Fruits and vegetables have their own set of preparation techniques. Here are the basics to get you going.

PREPARE ON THE WEEKEND

Salad Greens: Wash, sort, and dry greens.

Herbs: Wash, sort, and dry herbs.

Crudités (vegetables that can be eaten raw): Wash and cut fresh vegetables like sweet peppers, carrots, mushrooms, asparagus, and zucchini, into bite-sized pieces or slices.

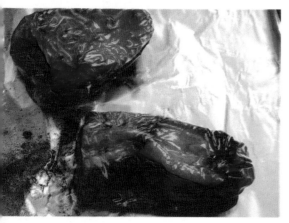

Roots & roastables: Winter squash, sweet potatoes, yams, beets, and red peppers can be cooked in advance.

- The best way to **roast beets** is to scrub them clean (leave skin on), put each beet on its own piece of foil, pour some olive oil over the top, and wrap the foil tight. Cook them at 350° F for 45 minutes to an hour depending on how big they are. Let cool and then use the foil to remove the skin – it will peel away easily. Cut them into pieces.

- To **roast a pepper**, wash it, put it on a piece of foil, pour some olive oil over the top, and cook it at 350° F for an hour. When done, wrap the edges of the foil together tightly for 20 minutes to let the pepper sweat; peel the skin off and remove the seeds.

- To **roast sweet potatoes** for Paleo Power Lunch recipes, peel, chop, toss in olive oil and cook at 350° F in a glass baking dish for 40 minutes or until tender.

Dressings and toppings can also be prepared and stored in serving-size containers on the weekend.

PREPARE ON THE DAY YOU'LL EAT THEM

Leafy greens that are better cooked should be cleaned and either steamed or wilted at the time you prepare your lunch.

Cabbage can be shredded in advance, but it is best to do it when making your lunch. The edges begin to brown and dry out after a day or two.

Fruit: Wash and cut fruit on the day you will use it. The sugars in fruits cause them to ripen and brown quickly; washing and cutting them accelerates this process.

Avocados, berries and stone fruit like peaches and nectarines are particularly delicate, and should be washed and cut just before you plan to use them.

STORING YOUR INGREDIENTS

There are three things to keep in mind when storing your lunch ingredients:

Freshness   **Visibility**   **Access**

For **freshness**, keep ingredients in air-tight containers. Bulk pantry items and meats in plastic bags or packages should be transferred to glass jars or BPA-free plastic food storage containers.

Visibility is about using clear containers, labeling them if you need to, and placing ingredients where you will see what you are looking for easily. Having things visible also means you are reminded to use them – don't let food wither away in the back of the fridge or not take your lunch because you can't find something.

Having lunch ingredients, as well as cooking supplies and lunch-packing gear, **accessible** makes it easier to put your lunch together quickly. Store all salad ingredients on the same shelf in the refrigerator (or cupboard for ingredients not requiring refrigeration). When you open the fridge, you'll know exactly where to find what you need. Pull it out at one go, grab the handfuls you need, and put it all back where you found it.

CHAPTER THREE

DRESSING IT UP

DELICIOUS DRESSINGS AND TOPPINGS

A Paleo Power Lunch can be thought of as a super salad. A power salad, if you will. It is not your typical salad, though. These are full-fledged, hearty meals that just happen to rest on a bed of greens. In my opinion, there's no better way to get your greens than to top them off with a succulent piece of meat, fresh veg, the light sweetness of fruit, some crunchy nuts or seeds – then pull it all together with a delicious dressing!

Paleo Power Lunches are each finished with a fresh, healthy dressing that complements and enhances an already-flavorful meal and with toppings to add crunch and flavor complexity to a relatively simple lunch.

ELEMENTS OF A HOMEMADE DRESSING

Making your own dressing may seem over-the-top at first. But, once you try it, you'll wonder how you ever considered commercial dressings to be good.

The key to an out-of-this-world salad dressing is in the combination of essential ingredients: the fat and acid which make up the base; the aromatic herbs and spices that add to the dressing's flavor; and the sweet and salty elements that round out the taste bud experience.

The great thing about making your own dressings, is that you are in control! No unnecessary fillers or sugars...just amazing flavor.

BODY AND BITE

Fat is essential! It makes food satisfying, rich and tasty. And, when balanced with the bright, biting acid of vinegar or citrus, it is a delight. Without these two elements – fats and acids, your Paleo Power Lunch is incomplete.

"To make a good salad is to be a brilliant diplomatist - the problem is entirely the same in both cases. To know how much oil one must mix with one's vinegar."

-- Oscar Wilde

AROMATIC ENHANCERS

Spices, fresh herbs, ginger and aromatic onions, garlic, and chives give your dressing distinct flavors, aromas, and freshness.

Fats	Acids	Aromatics
• Extra virgin olive oil • Avocado oil • Flax seed oil • Walnut oil • Warm bacon fat	• Fresh citrus juice (orange, lime, lemon, grapefruit) • Balsamic vinegar • Apple cider vinegar • Red or white wine vinegar • Sherry vinegar • Citrus zest • Coconut aminos	• Spices • Garlic, chives, shallots, & green onions • Ginger • Fresh herbs

CREAMINESS, COLOR AND COMPLEXITY

You can add creaminess to your dressing by adding ripe avocado or fatty, roasted nuts like macadamia nuts or walnuts. Roasted vegetables like beets and peppers, fresh cucumber or fresh tomato can add color and complexity to your dressing. Just blend them in.

HOLDING IT TOGETHER

To keep the oil and other liquids from separating, try using dry mustard powder to emulsify – or stabilize – the mixture. This extra ingredient will give the oil and liquid something to attach to so that they do not separate. Blending in fresh, leafy herbs will also help bind your dressing.

SWEET AND SALTY

Generally speaking, when it comes to a Paleo diet, salt and sweeteners – even natural ones – are best kept to a minimum. If you can't live without a little sweet and salt in your lunch, the dressing is the place to include them. Interestingly, once you are in the practice of eating foods without sweet and salty add-ins, your taste buds will be better able to appreciate the natural flavors of the foods you do eat.

THE SECRET DRESSING FORMULA REVEALED

The secret to great dressing boils down to numbers. Ratios specifically. Once you know them, you will be coming up with your own dressing recipes in no time flat.

In his book <u>Ratio</u>, Michael Ruhlman shares the goods:

BASIC VINAIGRETTE

=

3 parts fat +

1 part acid

BLENDED DRESSING

=

2 parts fat +

1 part acid +

1 part aromatic herbs, vegetables, creamy add-ins

These basic ratios are guidelines you can use to come up with your own combinations. **For a one-cup batch,** here are some more numbers to help you come up with your own recipes:

- Use a 4 to 1 fat:acid ratio if the acid you are using is very tart or strong – such as with lime juice. This will mellow the flavor.

- Add a teaspoon of dry mustard powder to vinaigrettes for flavor and to keep dressing from separating. Wasabi powder works well with citrus flavors if you prefer a little more kick.

- Add a teaspoon of fresh ginger or garlic, or a tablespoon of diced onion to the vinegar before blending in the oil.

- For color and flavor, blend 1/3 cup of chopped roasted beets, roasted red peppers, fresh tomatoes or cucumber with your other ingredients before adding in the oil.

- For sweetness, add a teaspoon of raw honey or 1/4 cup of roasted and pureed red beets to the mix. Replacing a small amount of your dressing's fat with apple juice can also take the edge off of a rich dressing.

MAKING AND STORING YOUR DRESSING

The temperature of ingredients and the process you use to mix your dressing make a difference in the result. Use room temperature ingredients when making your dressing; they hold together better than cold ingredients.

To naturally emulsify a dressing, combine all ingredients EXCEPT the oil in a small bowl or blender. Then, slowly whisk or blend the mixture while pouring the oil into the container in a thin stream.

The oil and liquid will begin to combine, causing the oil to pull away from the side of the bowl you are mixing it in. Soon it is thick and rich.

Whisking or blending fat and acid together too quickly may cause them to separate later. Go slow and steady. The more you blend or whisk your dressing, the thicker it will become.

Glass jars are ideal for storing your dressing. Canning, recycled food, and salad dressing jars are generally large enough to store a week's worth of dressing.

Recycled spice jars make nice containers for individual servings of dressing. You can also use BPA-free plastic food storage containers that hold 1/2 cup.

BATCH BASICS

Each recipe in this chapter makes approximately 1 cup of dressing, or six 2-Tablespoon servings.

Unlike store-bought dressings, these recipes do not include additives or preservatives; they will keep for about 1 week in the refrigerator before spoiling.

Dressings generally do not freeze well. If you don't eat all the dressing on your lunches, use the leftovers as a marinade, to add flavor to grilled meats, or on top of an omelet.

50-50 SINGLES

If you think you won't finish an entire batch of dressing, just whip up a quick single serving.

Don't worry about all of the extras – unless you want to. In fact, don't even worry about Ruhlman's ratios. Just go with a 50-50 fat to acid split + 1/4 teaspoon of a powdered spice to pull them together.

Balsamic Vinaigrette
1 1/2 Tbsp olive oil
1 1/2 Tbsp balsamic vinegar
1/4 tsp dry mustard powder

Citrus Dressing
1 1/2 Tbsp olive oil
1 1/2 Tbsp fresh-squeezed citrus juice
1/4 tsp wasabi powder

Curry Walnut Dressing
1 1/2 Tbsp walnut oil
1 1/2 Tbsp olive oil
1/4 tsp curry powder

To mix, just pour ingredients in a serving-size container, put the lid on, and shake it to blend everything together.

DRESSING RECIPES

BASIC BALSAMIC VINAIGRETTE

Makes ~1 cup

1/4 cup balsamic vinegar
1 clove garlic, minced
1 tsp dry mustard powder
1/4 tsp salt
1/4 tsp salt freshly ground black pepper
3/4 cup extra virgin olive oil

Using a whisk, beat all ingredients in a mixing bowl, except oil, until well combined. Slowly whisk in the oil.

BASIC CITRUS DRESSING

Makes ~1 cup. For this dressing you could use lemon, lime, orange (navel or blood), grapefruit, or a combination.

1/3 cup fresh-squeezed citrus juice
1 tsp dry mustard powder
1/4 tsp salt
1/4 tsp salt freshly ground black pepper
1/2 cup olive, flax seed, or avocado oil

Using a whisk, beat all ingredients in a mixing bowl, except oil, until well combined. Slowly whisk in the oil.

HONEY MUSTARD DRESSING

Makes ~1 cup

1/4 cup white wine vinegar or fresh-squeezed lemon juice
3 Tbsp raw honey
2 Tbsp dry mustard powder
1 clove garlic, minced
1/4 tsp salt
2/3 cup extra virgin olive oil

Using a whisk, beat all ingredients in a mixing bowl, except oil, until well combined. Slowly whisk in the oil.

CREAMY LEMON CHIVE DRESSING

Makes ~1 cup

1/3 cup fresh-squeezed lemon juice
2 Tbsp water
1 green onion, chopped
1 clove garlic, chopped
1 tsp dry mustard powder
1/4 tsp salt
Black pepper to taste
1/2 cup avocado oil or extra virgin olive oil
2 Tbsp chives, chopped

Combine all ingredients in a blender, except oil and chives. Slowly drizzle in the oil while the blender is going. Stir in chives when done.

CURRY & WALNUT DRESSING

Makes ~ 1 cup

1/4 cup lemon juice or apple cider vinegar
1 tsp minced ginger
1 clove garlic, minced
1 1/2 tsp mild curry powder
1/2 tsp salt
1/2 tsp raw honey (optional)
1/3 cup walnut oil
1/3 cup extra virgin olive oil

Using a whisk, beat all ingredients in a mixing bowl, except oil, until well combined. Slowly whisk in the oil.

ROASTED RED PEPPER VINAIGRETTE

Makes ~1 cup.

Roast up a pepper and add it to this gorgeous dressing for depth and richness. Cumin, chile powder and garlic add spiciness; the sweetness of the orange mellows them out...just a bit.

1/3 cup fresh-squeezed orange juice
Zest from half the orange (~1 tsp)
1 large roasted red pepper, de-seeded and skinned
1 clove garlic, chopped
1 tsp cumin
1/2 tsp chile powder (more if you like it hot!)
1/2 tsp salt
1/2 tsp freshly ground black pepper
1/2 cup extra virgin olive oil

Combine all ingredients. If it is too thick for your liking, add a tablespoon of water or orange juice if you have any left. Serve and enjoy.

Variations:

- Smoky Red Pepper Dressing: Use 1 tsp chipotle chile powder; remove cumin and regular chile powder from recipe.

- For a Mediterranean flare, use 1/3 cup of balsamic vinegar and 1 Tbsp of fresh basil in place of the orange juice and zest. Remove cumin and chile powder from recipe.

SPICY ALMOND DRESSING

Makes ~1 cup

1/4 cup fresh-squeezed lime juice
1/2 tsp salt
1 Tbsp minced onion
1/4 cup natural almond butter
1/2 tsp red pepper flakes (or more to taste)
1/2 cup flax seed or avocado oil
Optional: 1 tsp raw honey

Combine lime juice, salt, onion, and chili flakes in a blender. Add in almond butter and combine on slow speed. Keeping the blender going, slowly drizzle in the oil and blend until smooth

CREAMY TAHINI DRESSING

Makes ~ 3/4 cup

1/4 cup lemon juice
2 Tbsp tahini sesame paste
1 clove garlic, minced
1 1/2 tsp mild cumin powder
1/4 tsp smoked paprika
1/2 tsp salt
1/2 cup extra virgin olive oil
Optional: 1/2 tsp raw honey

Using a whisk, beat all ingredients in a mixing bowl, except oil, until well combined. Slowly whisk in the oil.

CREAMY AVOCADO CILANTRO DRESSING

Makes ~1 cup

1/2 medium, ripe avocado
1/2 cup packed fresh cilantro
1/4 cup orange juice
1/4 cup lime juice
1 green onion, chopped
1 clove garlic, chopped
1/2 tsp salt
1/4 cup extra virgin olive or avocado oil

Combine all ingredients in a blender, except oil. Slowly drizzle in the oil while the blender is going.

RED WINE VINAIGRETTE

Makes ~1 cup

1/4 cup red wine vinegar
1 tsp mustard powder
1/2 tsp salt
1/4 tsp salt freshly ground black pepper
3/4 cup extra virgin olive oil

Using a whisk, beat all ingredients in a mixing bowl, except oil, until well combined. Slowly whisk in the oil.

RED WINE VINAIGRETTE VARIATIONS

For a **Greek-style dressing**, mix in 1/4 teaspoon dried Mediterranean oregano leaves and 1 clove garlic, finely minced.

For an **Italian-style dressing**, use white wine vinegar instead of red. Add 1 teaspoon dried basil or Italian herb blend and 1 clove garlic, finely minced.

GINGER WASABI DRESSING

Makes ~1 cup

1 tsp wasabi powder (powdered horseradish)
1 tsp minced ginger
1 clove garlic, minced
1 tsp orange zest
1 Tbsp liquid coconut aminos
1/2 cup orange juice
1/2 cup extra virgin olive or avocado oil
Optional: 1 tsp toasted sesame seeds

Using a whisk, beat all ingredients in a mixing bowl, except oil, until well combined. Slowly whisk in the oil.

TOPPING IT OFF

A spoonful of toppings adds texture, contrasting flavor, and even some flare to your lunch.

RAW OR TOASTED NUTS
Almonds
Cashews
Hazelnuts
Macadamia nuts
Pecans
Pine nuts
Pistachios
Walnuts

RAW OR TOASTED SEEDS
Pepitas
Sesame seeds
Sunflower seeds

FRESH HERBS
Basil
Chives, minced
Cilantro
Dill
Fennel, sliced
Green onions, chopped
Mint
Parsley

THE OFT-OVERLOOKED
Roasted seaweed – nori works well
Unsweetened shredded coconut

CHAPTER FOUR

POWERFUL COMBINATIONS

PUTTING IT ALL TOGETHER

This chapter gets to the meat of the Paleo Power Lunch, so to speak. What at first glance is a salad, is really a powerful combination of delicious, filling ingredients. The flavors in the 26 power lunches are designed to complement each other, and they are just a sample of the versions you will soon be making for yourself. This is because Paleo Power Lunch is about strategy...not about prescriptive recipes.

This chapter provides flavor ideas and ways to create powerful lunches from scratch – regardless of what you have in the fridge.

THE MAKINGS OF A PALEO POWER LUNCH

The lunch recipes in this chapter follow a simple ingredient formula: greens, meat, vegetables, fruit, nuts or seeds, with a splash of dressing. Straightforward, simple, good eating.

This recipe did not make the cut, but it illustrates the point nicely.

CITRUS SEAFOOD POWER LUNCH

Tangy citrus complements the light and sweet flavor of shrimp and avocado in this lunch. When I run across fresh seafood medley or octopus at the market, I use them as a substitute or addition to the shrimp. Simple, filling, delicious.

2 cups spinach

3 ounces stir-fried shrimp or seafood medley

1/2 avocado, cut into chunks

1/2 orange, peeled and cut into chunks

2 Tbsp raw pepitas

Layer all ingredients in a lunch-sized food storage container.

Pack 2 Tbsp Basic Citrus Dressing (using lime juice) or 3 Tbsp Creamy Avocado Cilantro Dressing or Creamy Lemon Chive Dressing in a separate container.

MEAN GREEN NECTARINE & SHRIMP POWER LUNCH

This lunch is filled with lively green spinach, sprouts, and pepitas (or use shelled pistachios), and the bright, bold flavors of shrimp, red pepper, and nectarine. Oh, so good!

2 cups spinach

3 ounces poached or grilled shrimp

1/2 cup radish sprouts or pea sprouts

1/2 nectarine, chopped

1/4 cup chopped red pepper

2 Tbsp toasted (unsalted) pepitas or pistachios

Layer all ingredients in a lunch-sized food storage container.

Pack 3 Tbsp Creamy Avocado Cilantro Dressing or 2 Tbsp Basic Citrus Dressing (using lime juice) in a separate container.

TASTE OF THE TROPICS POWER LUNCH

Yum! Nuf said...almost. Make sure your mango is ripe to get the best flavor. The sweet mango tastes amazing with the creamy avocado and cashews. And, of course, shrimp and coconut just scream of the tropics.

2 cups spring greens

3 ounces poached or grilled shrimp

1/2 mango, chopped

1/2 avocado, chopped

2 Tbsp unsalted cashews, raw or toasted

1 tsp unsweetened, shredded coconut

Layer all ingredients in a lunch-sized food storage container.

Pack 2 Tbsp Basic Citrus Dressing (using lime juice) or Creamy Avocado Cilantro Dressing or Creamy Lemon Chive Dressing in a separate container.

FISH TACO POWER LUNCH

It's like a fish taco without the tortilla! Spice up your fish with a little chile powder for extra flavor.

2 cups thinly shredded Napa cabbage or pre-cut cole slaw mix

3 ounces pan-fried tilapia

1/2 cup cherry or chopped tomatoes

2 Tbsp fresh cilantro

2 Tbsp pepitas

1 Tbsp red onion

- Layer all ingredients in a lunch-sized food storage container.

  Pack 3 Tbsp Creamy Avocado Cilantro Dressing in a separate container.

SUPER POWER LUNCH

Exert your super powers by crushing the kale to break down the fibers. Later in the day, these super foods will return the favor and power you. Be forewarned: the strong flavors in this power lunch are not for everyone.

2 cups sliced kale, massaged with your hands

3 ounces broiled salmon

1/2 cup chopped roasted sweet potato

1/4 cup blueberries

1 sliced hard-boiled egg

2 Tbsp chopped walnuts

Layer all ingredients in a lunch-sized food storage container.

Pack 2 Tbsp of Basic Citrus Dressing or Honey Mustard Dressing in a separate container.

SESAME SALMON POWER LUNCH

Salmon is strong-tasting fish. The fresh greens, asparagus, and cukes keep it from feeling too heavy in the middle of the day. Sweet oranges, sesame seeds, and a spicy dressing kick the flavors up a notch.

2 cups spring greens

3 ounces broiled salmon, flaked

3-4 asparagus stalks, cut into 1" pieces

1/2 of a Cara Cara or Mandarin orange, cut into pieces

1/4 cup sliced cucumber

1 Tbsp diced green onion

1 tsp sesame seeds

Layer all ingredients in a lunch-sized food storage container.

Pack 2 Tbsp Ginger Wasabi Dressing in a separate container.

TUNA NIÇOISE POWER LUNCH

Tuna Niçoise originates in the South of France. Purists proclaim that no cooked vegetable should be introduced to the mix, and that a smattering of tinned anchovies should be layered on top – add them if you have them; they add great flavor!

2 cups spring greens

3 ounces poached or grilled albacore tuna steak, flaked

1/2 cup cherry or chopped tomatoes

1/2 cup chopped red pepper

3-4 asparagus stalks, cut into 1" pieces

1 sliced hard-boiled egg

2 Tbsp Kalamata olives, pitted

1 Tbsp diced green onion

Layer all ingredients in a lunch-sized food storage container.

Pack 2 Tbsp Honey Mustard Dressing in a separate container.

NORSEMAN'S POWER LUNCH

The rich flavors of smoked salmon and arugula are balanced by crisp cucumber and dill in this hearty lunch. You can substitute grilled or broiled salmon for smoked.

2 cups arugula or spring greens

2 ounces of smoked salmon, cut into bite-sized pieces

1/2 cup chopped cucumber

1/2 cup cherry or grape tomatoes

1 sliced hard-boiled egg

1 Tbsp diced red onion

1 Tbsp fresh dill fronds

Layer all ingredients in a lunch-sized food storage container.

Pack 2 Tbsp Basic Citrus Dressing (using lemon juice) in a separate container.

COBB POWER LUNCH

This is the original odd-and-ends salad, though the only point that people agree upon is that it was invented by one Robert Howard Cobb. It works great with leftovers, tastes amazing, and is incredibly filling.

2 cups chopped romaine lettuce

3 ounces grilled chicken, cut into chunks

2 strips cooked bacon, crumbled

1 hard-boiled egg, chopped

1/2 cup cherry tomatoes, halved

1/2 avocado, cut into chunks

Layer all ingredients in a lunch-sized food storage container.

Pack 2 Tbsp Red Wine Vinaigrette or 3 Tbsp Creamy Lemon Chive Dressing in a separate container.

MEDITERRANEAN CHOPPED LUNCH

Chunky pieces of grilled meat, cucumbers, green peppers and tomatoes make this a hearty salad for sure. But add in the onion, oregano, and a tangy dressing, and you have a meal that is also delicious and satisfying.

2 cups red or green-leafed lettuce, chopped

3 ounces grilled chicken or lamb, chopped

1/2 cup cherry or chopped tomatoes

1/2 cup chopped cucumber

1/2 cup chopped green pepper

1 Tbsp diced red onion

1 tsp fresh oregano leaves

Layer all ingredients in a lunch-sized food storage container.

Pack 2 Tbsp Basic Citrus Dressing (using lemon juice) or Creamy Tahini Dressing in a separate container.

CHICKEN LOOSE IN THE GARDEN LUNCH

This is a garden-variety lunch, packed with fresh veggies. Add a tablespoon of raw sunflower seeds for extra flavor and crunch.

2 cups spinach

3 ounces grilled chicken, chopped

1/4 cup radish sprouts or pea sprouts

1/4 cup cherry or chopped tomatoes

1/4 cup matchstick carrots

1/4 cup chopped cucumber

1/4 cup sliced celery

1/4 cup sliced mushrooms

Layer all ingredients in a lunch-sized food storage container.

Pack 2 Tbsp of Roasted Red Pepper Vinaigrette in a separate container.

SWEETHEART SALAD

Did you know that strawberries and asparagus are considered aphrodisiacs? In this salad, they make a delicious match against the bold flavor of arugula, red onion, and balsamic vinegar.

2 cups arugula

3 ounces grilled chicken, chopped

4 large strawberries, sliced

5-6 stalks of asparagus, cut into 1" lengths

1 tsp red onion, chopped (a little packs a whollop)

1/2 cup pecans

Layer all ingredients in a lunch-sized food storage container.

Pack 2 Tbsp Basic Balsamic Vinaigrette in a separate container.

CURRIED WALNUT CHICKEN LUNCH

This is one of my favorite sweet and savory combinations – walnuts, apples, chicken and curry. The carrots and celery add crunch. Toss in a handful of chopped red pepper for additional vegetables and flavor.

2 cups spinach

3 ounces grilled chicken, chopped

1/2 cup matchstick carrots

1/2 cup sliced celery

1/2 green apple, chopped

2 Tbsp walnuts

1 Tbsp raisins

1 tsp diced chives

Layer all ingredients in a lunch-sized food storage container.

Pack 2 Tbsp Curry & Walnut Dressing in a separate container.

ASIAN CHICKEN SALAD POWER LUNCH

This lunch tastes great with FRESH oranges - not the kind you find in a can. Go for in-season Cara Cara or Mandarin oranges for best flavor! And the carrots are optional - add them in if you like a little extra color.

2 cups finely shredded Napa cabbage or pre-packaged cole slaw mix

3 ounces grilled chicken, chopped

1/2 cup chopped red pepper

1/2 orange, cut into pieces

2 Tbsp slivered almonds

1 Tbsp diced green onion

1 tsp sesame seeds

Layer all ingredients in a lunch-sized food storage container.

Pack 2 Tbsp Ginger Wasabi Dressing or Spicy Almond Dressing in a separate container.

SWEET POTATO PECAN POWER LUNCH

This power lunch with a Southern flare – think grilled meat and sweet potato pie – has become a favorite in our household. And, besides, who doesn't love a little bacon?

2 cups spinach

2 ounces grilled chicken, chopped

2 pieces of cooked bacon, crumbled

1/4 cup chopped roasted sweet potato (yams, actually)

2 Tbsp pecan pieces

1 Tbsp red onion

Layer all ingredients in a lunch-sized food storage container.

Pack 2 Tbsp Honey Mustard Dressing in a separate container.

MANGO MACADAMIA MADNESS LUNCH

Mmm, mmm, mmm! Yeah – it's good. Watercress, like arugula, is peppery and strong. By using sweet and mild-flavored ingredients like mango, macadamia, and even avocado, you wind up with balanced flavors that are just plain good together.

2 cups watercress or arugula

3 ounces grilled pork or chicken, chopped

1/2 mango, chopped

1/2 avocado, chopped

2 Tbsp chopped macadamia nuts

Layer all ingredients in a lunch-sized food storage container.

Pack 2 Tbsp Basic Citrus Dressing (using lime juice) or even Curry & Walnut Dressing - for a very different kind of taste experience - in a separate container.

LEMON BLACKBERRY BURST LUNCH

This is the lunch that started it all. In the dead of winter, wanting something colorful to go with a leftover pork chop, I threw it together with a handful of berries, seeds, and avocado. It's earthy, but light. Add a handful of raw mushrooms for more vegetables.

2 cups spinach

3 ounces pan-fried pork loin chop, sliced

1/2 avocado, cut into chunks

1/2 cup fresh blackberries

2 Tbsp raw pepitas

Layer all ingredients in a lunch-sized food storage container.

Pack 3 Tbsp Creamy Lemon Chive Dressing in a separate container.

FENNELICIOUS ROAST PORK LUNCH

Fennel and pork are soul mates. They are great together. The celery, pears, and hazelnuts give this bright, flavorful salad some crunch and unique flavor.

2 cups red leafed lettuce

3 ounces roasted pork loin, chopped

1/4 cup sliced fennel bulb

1/4 cup sliced celery

1/2 bosc pear, cut into chunks

2 Tbsp chopped hazelnuts (toasted if you like)

1 tsp chopped chives

Layer all ingredients in a lunch-sized food storage container.

Pack 2 Tbsp of Basic Citrus Dressing or Honey Mustard Dressing in a separate container.

NOT SO-STUFFED PIG LUNCH

While this roast pork lunch does have an apple, you won't feel stuffed by it. This lighter lunch is peppered with spicy arugula and honey mustard dressing but tempered by celery and walnuts.

2 cups arugula

3-4 ounces roasted pork loin, chopped

1/2 green apple, chopped

1/4 cup sliced celery

2 Tbsp chopped walnuts

Layer all ingredients in a lunch-sized food storage container.

Pack 2 Tbsp Honey Mustard Dressing in a separate container.

THAI ONE ON FOR LUNCH

This lunch is a new favorite. It uses pomelos (AKA pummelos) – a South East Asian citrus fruit that is delicious in season and actually very easy to use. Peel the thick rind, separate the segments, peel the skin off of the fruit pieces inside, and voila! Top this lunch off with unsweetened, shredded coconut.

2 cups red-leafed lettuce

3 ounces roasted pork loin, chopped

1/2 cup chopped red pepper

1/2 cup pomelo pieces

1/2 cup chopped cucumber

1 Tbsp diced green onion

1 Tbsp minced fresh mint

1 Tbsp minced fresh cilantro

2 Tbsp unsalted cashews, raw or toasted

Layer all ingredients in a lunch-sized food storage container.

Pack 2 Tbsp Basic Citrus Dressing (using lime juice) or Spicy Almond Dressing in a separate container.

BETTER WITH BEETS

This lunch blends the flavor of fresh-roasted beets served with earthy walnuts, dill, and the tangy sweetness of oranges to make an "I love it" kind of lunch. If in season, use blood oranges in this lunch.

2 cups arugula

3 ounces roasted pork, chopped

1/2 cup roasted beets, chopped

3 orange slices, chopped

10 walnut halves

1-2 Tbsp chopped dill

Layer all ingredients in a lunch-sized food storage container.

Pack 2 Tbsp Basic Balsamic Vinaigrette or Basic Citrus Dressing (using orange juice) in a separate container.

FAJITA POWER LUNCH

If you like fajitas, you'll love this Tex-Mex style meal. It tastes best when you pan fry the steak, peppers, and onions together. Cook them the night before or first thing in the morning and then put them in a separate storage container to keep the hot foods from wilting your fresh veggies.

2 cups spinach

3 ounces of stir-fried strips of steak

1/2 red pepper, cut into strips (cook with steak for best flavor)

2 Tbsp onion, chopped

1/2 avocado, cut into chunks

1/2 cup cherry tomatoes, cut in halves

2 Tbsp raw pepitas

Layer all ingredients in a lunch-sized food storage container.

Pack 3 Tbsp Creamy Avocado Cilantro Dressing or Creamy Lemon Chive Dressing in a separate container.

SAMURAI POWER LUNCH

Get all of the flavor, but not the price tag of a Japanese steak house lunch experience with this hearty lunch fit for a Samurai. Crunchy, refreshing, yet filling.

2 cups spring greens

3 ounces pan-fried or grilled steak, sliced

1/4 cup sliced cucumber

1/4 cup sliced celery

1/4 cup matchstick carrots

2 radishes, sliced

1 Tbsp diced green onion

1 tsp sesame seeds

Layer all ingredients in a lunch-sized food storage container.

Pack 2 Tbsp Ginger Wasabi Dressing in a separate container.

PUT A STEAK IN IT LUNCH

Go back to basics with this straightforward steak and garden vegetable lunch. The acidity of the red wine or balsamic complement the flavors beautifully.

2 cups red leafed lettuce, chopped

3 ounces grilled steak, sliced

1/2 cup cherry tomatoes, halved

1/2 cup green pepper, chopped

1/4 cup raw mushrooms, sliced

1 Tbsp red onion, finely chopped

1 Tbsp raw sunflower seeds

Layer all ingredients in a lunch-sized food storage container.

Pack 2 Tbsp Red Wine or Basic Balsamic Vinaigrette in a separate container.

MOROCCAN LUNCH

Sweet and spicy, rich and smoky – that's what you get in this Moroccan-inspired lunch when combined with the Roasted Red Pepper Vinaigrette. The raisins and pine nuts can easily be replaced (or even left out altogether) with chopped, dried apricots and walnuts if you happen to have those on hand instead.

2 cups red leafed lettuce, chopped

3 ounces grilled steak, sliced

1/4 cup chopped roasted sweet potato

1/2 cup tomatoes, chopped

2 Tbsp diced red onion

1 Tbsp raisins

1 tsp pine nuts

1 tsp minced fresh mint

Layer all ingredients in a lunch-sized food storage container.

Pack 2 Tbsp Roasted Red Pepper Vinaigrette or Creamy Tahini Dressing in a separate container.

HOME ON THE RANGE LUNCH

Bison is a naturally pasture-raised animal that is both healthy and rich-tasting. The fresh and sweet flavors of mint, cilantro, and cantaloupe are a perfect combination.

2 cups spring greens

3 ounces stir-fried bison stew meat

1/2 cup cantaloupe, scooped or chopped

1/2 cup red pepper, chopped

1 Tbsp red onion

1 tsp minced fresh mint

1 tsp minced fresh cilantro

Layer all ingredients in a lunch-sized food storage container.

Pack 2 Tbsp of Basic Citrus Dressing or Roasted Red Pepper Vinaigrette in a separate container.

QUICK CROSS REFERENCE

Lunch	Dressing Suggestions	Techniques Used
Citrus Seafood Power Lunch, 58	Basic Citrus Dressing (using lime juice), 46 Creamy Avocado Cilantro Dressing, 51 Creamy Lemon Chive Dressing, 48	Poach Shrimp, 31
Mean Green Nectarine & Shrimp Power Lunch, 59	Creamy Avocado Cilantro Dressing, 51 Basic Citrus Dressing (using lime juice), 46	Poach Shrimp, 31
Taste of the Tropics Power Lunch, 60	Basic Citrus Dressing (using lime juice), 46 Creamy Avocado Cilantro Dressing, 51 Creamy Lemon Chive Dressing, 48	Poach Shrimp, 31
Fish Taco Power Lunch, 61	Creamy Avocado Cilantro Dressing, 51	Pan-fry Tilapia, 33
Super Power Lunch, 62	Basic Citrus Dressing, 46 Honey Mustard Dressing, 47	Broil Salmon, 29 Roast Sweet Potato, 36 Hard-boil Eggs, 35
Sesame Salmon Power Lunch, 63	Ginger Wasabi Dressing, 52	Broil Salmon, 29
Tuna Niçoise Power Lunch, 64	Honey Mustard Dressing, 47	Poach Tuna, 31 Hard-boil Eggs, 35
Norseman's Power Lunch, 65	Basic Citrus Dressing, 46	Hard-boil Eggs, 35
Cobb Power Lunch, 66	Red Wine Vinaigrette, 52 Creamy Lemon Chive Dressing, 48	Grill Chicken, 30 Hard-boil Eggs, 35
Mediterranean Chopped Lunch, 67	Basic Citrus Dressing, 46 Creamy Tahini Dressing, 50	Grill Chicken, 30
Chicken Loose in the Garden Lunch, 68	Roasted Red Pepper Vinaigrette, 49	Grill Chicken, 30
Sweetheart Salad , 69	Basic Balsamic Vinaigrette, 46	Grill Chicken, 30

Curried Walnut Chicken Lunch, 70	Curry & Walnut Dressing, 47	Grill Chicken, 30
Asian Chicken Salad Power Lunch, 71	Ginger Wasabi Dressing, 52 Spicy Almond Dressing, 50	Grill Chicken, 30
Sweet Potato Pecan Power Lunch, 72	Honey Mustard Dressing, 47	Grill Chicken, 30 Roast Sweet Potato, 36
Mango Macadamia Madness Lunch, 73	Basic Citrus Dressing (using lime juice), 46 Curry & Walnut Dressing, 47	Grill Chicken or Pork, 30
Lemon Blackberry Burst Lunch, 74	Creamy Lemon Chive Dressing, 48	Pan-fry Pork Chop, 33
Fennelicious Roast Pork Lunch, 75	Basic Citrus Dressing, 46 Honey Mustard Dressing, 47	Roast Pork Loin, 32
Not-So-Stuffed Pig Lunch, 76	Honey Mustard Dressing, 47	Roast Pork Loin, 32
Thai One On for Lunch, 77	Basic Citrus Dressing (using lime juice), 46 Spicy Almond Dressing, 50	Roast Pork Loin, 32
Better with Beets, 78	Basic Balsamic Vinaigrette, 46 Basic Citrus Dressing (using blood orange juice), 46	Roast Pork Loin, 32 Roast Beets, 36
Fajita Lunch, 79	Creamy Avocado Cilantro Dressing, 51 Creamy Lemon Chive Dressing, 48	Stir-fry Beef & Veg, 34
Samurai Power Lunch, 80	Ginger Wasabi Dressing, 52	Pan-fry Steak, 33
Put a Steak in it Lunch, 81	Red Wine Vinaigrette, 52 Basic Balsamic Vinaigrette, 46	Grill Steak, 30
Moroccan Lunch, 82	Roasted Red Pepper Vinaigrette, 49 Creamy Tahini Dressing, 50	Grill Steak, 30
Home on the Range Lunch, 83	Basic Citrus Dressing, 46 Roasted Red Pepper Vinaigrette, 49	Stir-fry Bison, 34

MIXING THINGS UP

If you don't have all of the ingredients for a lunch recipe listed in this book or don't like one of the ingredients, don't worry. Just substitute.

Remove the thing you don't like, add in something else you do, make it vegetarian, or make up your own mix - anything goes!

My favorite lunch – and the way I first developed this idea, in fact, is by making Odds and Ends Lunches (not shown here because they change every time I make them). Simply open your fridge and cupboards. Use whatever fresh, healthy ingredients you have.

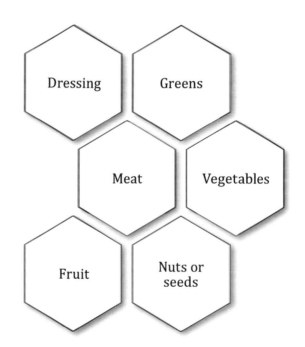

Odds and Ends Lunches are an excuse to steam those broccoli florets that have been sitting there for just about too long, to use up leftovers from the grill or crockpot, or maybe even to dabble in a dressing that uses a spice you've never tried.

Mix it up! Make it work for you.

DECONSTRUCTING AND REBUILDING

The inspiration for many of the Paleo Power Lunch recipes come from cuisines or dishes I've eaten that weren't originally in this format. Instead, they were sandwiches, soups, whole meals, or flavor combinations I'd come across in my travels.

That is the great thing about them, because it means that you can use the Paleo Power Lunch formula to come up with your own favorite flavor combinations, too.

Sure, you can experiment. But, you can also deconstruct. In other words, look to meals you've had at favorite restaurants or on the road, and pull together lunches that reflect the core flavors of that meal while respecting Paleo dietary principles. Use greens instead of bread, pull the sugars, work with the basics, and go from there.

Here are a handful of deconstruction examples to get you started:

- Bahn Mi Vietnamese Sandwich: A combination of roasted pork belly, grilled pork, grilled chicken, canned sardines in tomato sauce, and/or fried eggs. Add fresh cucumber slices, cilantro, matchstick carrots, daikon radish slices, and a bit of jalapeno. Top with Basic Citrus Dressing (using lime juice).

- Dressed Louisiana Po Boy Sandwich: Shredded pork, beef, fish, or shrimp on shredded cabbage or lettuce, with tomatoes, onion, pickles, and Honey Mustard dressing.

- Southwest Chicken Bacon Sandwich: Grilled chicken, bacon, fresh cilantro, red onion, and Roasted Red Pepper Vinaigrette (using chipotle variation) on a bed of romaine.

- Tempura Undone: Shrimp, roasted sweet potato, sliced onions, carrots, and zucchini, with Ginger Wasabi Dressing.

- Chicken Tagine: Shredded chicken, chopped apricot, roasted sweet potato, red onion, cilantro, pine nuts or pistachios and Roasted Red Pepper Vinaigrette.

CHAPTER FIVE

PACKS AND SNACKS

GETTING YOUR LUNCH TO WORK

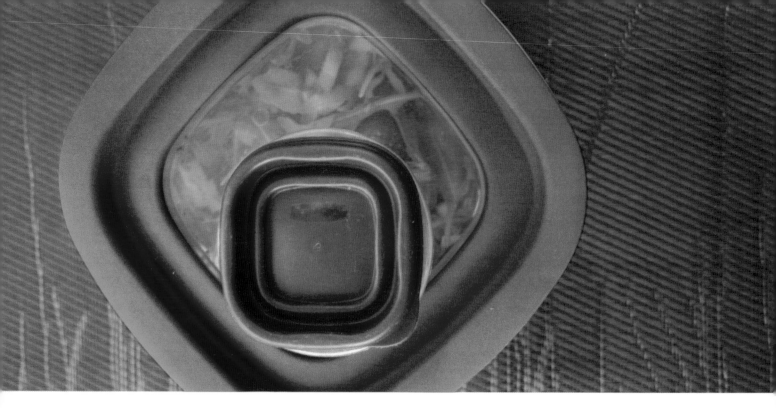

I know how easy it is to skip making lunch and to walk out the door empty-handed. So making your own lunch has to be a priority so it actually makes it to work with you.

Making a specific lunch combination work *for* you is the other side of the coin. All of the lunch recipes I've provided are intended as ideas. Start with them and then create your own. By using what you have and what you like, and by keeping things simple, you'll look forward to what you've brought for lunch.

Having the right snacks to go along with your lunch makes things all the better – you have food if you need it and it is food you can trust is good for you.

THE SCIENCE OF PACKING

Packing your lunch requires a bit of practice and the right equipment.

PUTTING YOUR PALEO POWER LUNCH TOGETHER

If you planned ahead and prepared ingredients on the weekend, putting your Paleo Power Lunch together before heading out for the day should be a snap. Here's how to do it:

1. In the morning before going to work, pull out the ingredients you'll need for the lunch recipe you are making. If you are in the habit of rushing around in the morning, make your lunch the night before you need it so you don't run out of time and decide not to bother.

2. Place all lunch ingredients into lidded containers. Make sure one of the containers is large enough to hold all of your Power Lunch fixings when you combine them. If you prefer to reheat your meat, poultry or seafood before adding it to your meal, simply put it in its own container. If you want to cut your avocado or fruit at work to keep them from browning, take them whole.

3. Pour one serving of dressing into a small container. For each recipe, I recommend 2 tablespoons for a thinner dressing, 3 for the creamier vegetable and herb-heavy dressings. Keep your lunch and dressing separated until you are ready to eat, prevents greens from wilting.

4. Place your food containers into a cooler or lunch bag. This includes your lunch and dressing, **as well as** snacks and water. Snacks and water can make a huge difference in your day, by preventing hunger, keeping energy high, and reducing cravings.

5. At lunch, reheat any ingredients you want to, toss them together with the fresh ingredients and dressing, and eat!

> **Quick Tip:**
>
> Homemade dressings tend to thicken in the fridge. Consider putting the dressing on your desk when you first get to work so it warms to room temperature by the time you eat lunch. Then, you can easily shake your dressing up and drizzle or spoon it over your Paleo Power Lunch.

FINDING THE PERFECT LUNCH BOX

Firstly, you'll want to buy a lunch box that does what you need it to do. Here are some things to consider:

Cost: You can buy a decent adult lunch box these days for anywhere from $5.00 for a basic cloth lunch sack with a Velcro enclosure to $65.00 for an insulated lunch bag with stainless steel thermal food storage containers inside.

Style: If you carry your lunch around in the car all day, how your lunch box looks may not be as important as how it functions. If you are taking it into professional meetings or want it to reflect

your personality, though, style might just matter. Fortunately, lunch boxes can be retro, professional, pretty, rugged, designer, or just plain, well, plain. And, they can be bags, totes, coolers, boxes, and even look like purses.

Functionality: Find a lunch box that functions in the ways you need it to. For example:

- Insulation – does it keep food cold enough if you can't put your lunch in the fridge?

- Size and shape – does it easily hold the amount of food and liquid that you need and the types of food containers you use? Will ice packs also fit if you need them to keep food cold?

- Hygiene – is it easily washable, either by wiping or throwing it in with the laundry?

- Sturdiness – Are the enclosures solid, do the materials seem sturdy, and does it look like the stitches (if there are any) will hold up over time?

LUNCH CONTAINER IDEAS

Some lunch boxes come with their own food containers, water bottle, thermos, and utensils. Having containers that are specifically designed for your lunch box makes packing easier, but only if they hold the amount of food you need and leave room for other goodies in the bag. Check the lids, too – some containers are cheaply made and can leak.

You can also buy your own containers or use recycled containers like canning jars with good seals. Look for containers that are easily cleanable; stackable (for space savings and fit); BPA-free plastic, stainless steel, or glass; and, if you are going to reheat foods, microwave-safe.

THE ART OF SNACKING

Lunch is only part of the equation when you are planning for a day's worth of eating away from home. If you get hungry before leaving work or need foods to fuel or recover from a workout away from home, snacks can help you stave off hunger, keep your metabolism revved up, and stop you from eating things you are trying to avoid.

Your snacks should vary depending on what you have planned for the day. Here are some questions to think about when deciding what to pack:

- **Time and energy needs:** What kind of day are you facing? Will you be gone longer than usual or are you stopping at the gym and need fuel or recovery food?

- **Ease:** Are you going to need grab-and-go snacks that are clean and easy to eat in your car, or small-and-discrete treats that you can pull from a purse, jacket pocket, or briefcase during a meeting?

- **Variety:** Do your snacks complement – rather than duplicate – your lunch? For example, if your lunch includes calorie-dense ingredients like nuts or avocados, you might want to take other foods for snacks. While monitoring what you eat is one reason to do this, avoiding boredom with your food is another – mix up what you eat each day.

- **Flavor:** Snacks should be quick to prepare and easy to grab on the go, AND they should taste good. Fresh fruit and vegetables are obvious, clean and wholesome snack choices, but they are deliciously transformed with toppings! Liven then up with a Paleo dip, nut butters, raw cacao nibs, a sprinkle of cinnamon or other spices, or some fresh mint.

Pack what you need to get you through the day – however long and crazy it is.

COOLER COMPANIONS

Try packing some of these snack options to keep you going:

- 2 Tbsp almond butter and a banana or apple

- A hard-boiled egg with black pepper and a sprinkle of toasted sesame seeds

- Paleo hummus – make your own hummus and use raw zucchini or roasted beets, peppers, pumpkin or sweet potato in place of the chickpeas.

KEEPING A STASH

Back in the day, I had a drawer full of snacks that could rival your best grocery store selection... from soup to nuts, literally. I still find snack bars in my purse and back pack that have been there a while. Fortunately, I've found only one forgotten banana - right before it became a problem.

Even if you are intentionally spacing your meals farther apart or working to eliminate snacking altogether, an emergency supply of food is not a bad thing.

Keeping snacks where you need them can mean the difference between eating something good for you and either going hungry or eating something you shouldn't. Store shelf-stable snacks in your desk, a work bag, and maybe even your car to make sure you have back-up.

- A piece of fresh fruit or handful of raw vegetables

- 2 lettuce wraps with shredded meat or vegetables inside

- 1/2 cup of fresh trail mix – instead of dried fruit, use fresh black, blue and raspberries with 2 Tbsp of nuts and seeds.

- Paleo muhammara – blend roasted red peppers with toasted walnuts, garlic, a bit of lemon juice, and cumin. A touch of pomegranate molasses or juice adds a bit of traditional sweetness.

- Guacamole – sprinkle the top with lemon juice to keep it from turning brown.

- A serving of sauerkraut or other pickled vegetables. If you can make your own, great. If not, look for pickled goods that do not include sugar. Mmmm!

- Serving-sized frittatas – Make frittatas by whisking together 3 eggs, 1/2 cup chopped, cooked meat, 1/2 cup of sautéed veggies and herbs, and 2 tablespoons of homemade dressing. Pour equal amounts of mix into 4 muffin cups and bake at 350° F for 18 minutes. Refrigerate them and pull just one or two out the morning you need them.

- Three 1-ounce meatballs – Mix ground beef, pork or turkey with chopped onion and garlic. Roll the meat into 1-ounce balls. Pan-fry the meatballs, let cool, then freeze until the night before you need them. Refrigerate to thaw and reheat at work.

- A cup of homemade soup – pureed vegetable soups are easy and tasty – or bone broth

- An 8-oz container of coconut water or kombucha

- Roasted seaweed snacks

- Half a can of albacore tuna or sardines with a squeeze of lemon juice and some chopped chives

WATER IS ESSENTIAL

Drinking water is the best way to keep you hydrated. Staying hydrated helps your kidneys function properly, regulates your system (you know what I mean), keeps your muscles toned, and can even keep your appetite in check.

But, drinking *enough* water is a challenge – especially if you are used to drinking fluids that are filled with artificial flavors and sugars. Your taste buds just aren't used to water.

Whether or not drinking water comes naturally to you, here are some ideas for making sure you stay hydrated all day:

- Fill a 16-ounce bottle with water and drink it on the way to work. Finish it before you get there.

- Pack a couple of full 32-ounce bottles (1 quart each) of water and keep one with you at all times throughout the day. Try to drink the first one by the time you finish lunch and the second by the end of the day. This is helpful if you have a tough time remembering to drink water or don't like heading to the drinking fountain every half hour.

- Set an alarm to remind yourself that it's time to grab a drink. Drink as much as you can.

- Need flavor? Add sliced citrus fruit, strawberry, or cucumber to your drink, or a sprig of fresh mint.

- Keep a drinking glass, quart-sized mason jar, stainless steel water bottle, or BPA-free plastic bottle at work, just in case you forget to bring a bottle with you. Wash it regularly.

A FINAL NOTE

Any time you make a change in the way you eat, getting comfortable with new habits can take time and energy. This can be a challenge when working from home, with access to food all day. It's even more of a challenge when away from home with less control of food you have access to!

Adjusting to new flavors can also take time, especially if you have been used to eating bland or very sweet and salty foods. Like with other muscles in your body, if you don't exercise your taste buds and shock them with new flavors now and then, they atrophy. By giving your taste buds a workout that includes different flavors, textures, and sensations, they will begin to appreciate the nuances in the new foods you eat.

I hope, by now, you've seen that with a few good strategies, cooking skills, and getting into the practice of packing your lunch, an often-forgotten but important meal, you can take control of what you eat during the day in a delicious, healthy, and easy way.

RESOURCES

RECOMMENDED READING

BOOKS

The Butcher's Guide to Well-Raised Meat: How to Buy, Cut, and Cook Great Beef, Lamb, Pork, Poultry, and More by Joshua and Jessica Applestone of Fleisher's Grass-fed & Organic Meats, and Alexandra Zissu

The Flavor Bible: The Essential Guide to Culinary Creativity, Based on the Wisdom of America's Most Imaginative Chefs by Karen Page and Andrew Dornenburg

The Locavore's Handbook: The Busy Person's Guide to Eating Local on a Budget by Leda Meredith

The Omnivore's Dilemma by Michael Pollan

The Paleo Diet: Lose Weight and Get Healthy by Eating the Food You Were Designed to Eat by Loren Cordain

The Paleo Solution: The Original Human Diet by Robb Wolf

It Starts with Food by Dallas Hartwig and Melissa Hartwig

WEBSITES

Seafood Watch from the Monterey Bay Aquarium The Monterey Bay Aquarium Seafood Watch program helps consumers and businesses make choices for healthy oceans. Their recommendations indicate which seafood items are "Best Choices," "Good Alternatives," and which ones you should "Avoid." They offer resources on their website, a printable pocket guide, and a mobile app. Find them at: http://www.montereybayaquarium.org/cr/seafoodwatch.aspx

U.S. Wellness Meats Great source of grassland meat and poultry. http://www.grasslandbeef.com

RECIPES & HOW-TO'S: A COMPLETE LIST

POWER LUNCH RECIPES

INDEX

GRATITUDE

To Chiao-ih Hui, for organizing delicious test-kitchen days and starting down the food writing path with me, as well as to the rest of the "crew" for their dining companionship and excellent taste.

To my former co-workers who oohed and aahed over my lunch each day – if you hadn't, I might not have known I was on to something.

To Vanessa Chang, food-passionate, cookbook-editing, Cross Fit enthusiast for digging the book's concept and for encouraging its Paleo focus.

To Melissa Joulwan for making her mark on the world of self-publishing and being willing to share her experience and advice with me.

For creating room and motivation to write, thanks go to Amy Scott, nomad editor extraordinaire, and the Ticket to Write group participants.

I am also grateful for the amazing friends, supporters, guides, and critical eaters in my life. I constantly learn from and am inspired by you.

ABOUT THE AUTHOR

Stormy Sweitzer, MPH, is founder of Maoomba, a company dedicated to real food education, exploration, and community.

When food allergies and sensitivities began wreaking havoc on Stormy's health, she began a journey that led her to new ways of cooking, eating, and living her life. Today she writes and teaches about delicious, real foods that are naturally free of common allergens and prioritize whole, nutrient-rich ingredients.

Stormy draws on her curiosity, 20+ years of cooking, kitchen experimentation, and systems thinking to share recipes and kitchen strategies that take time, health, and budgetary constraints into consideration without sacrificing flavor. Her motto: the food we eat needs to fit into our lives, not the other way around.

For weekly real food tips, recipes, and stories, sign up for the Maoomba newsletter at Maoomba.com. If you have questions about this book or suggestions for future resources, please feel free to send Stormy an email at info@maoomba.com.